Player's Handbook

A Study Guide for

In His Grip
Foundations for Life and Golf

Jim Sheard, Ph.D. and Wally Armstrong

Jim Sheard, Ph.D.
& Wally Armstrong

Player's Handbook

for

IN HIS GRIP:
Foundations for Life and Golf

SECTION I

"ON THE TEE"

SECTION II

"IN THE FAIRWAY"

Section III

"HELP FOR THE HAZARDS"

Section IV

"ON THE GREEN"

Appendix

Introduction

LIFE AND GOLF

Both golf and life require a solid foundation. Without a solid base our life and golf swing are on shifting sand. When the winds of challenge come, you will be gripped by the turmoil of pressure, fear, anger, and failure. A solid foundation gives us the opportunity to plan, learn from past experiences, and prepare ourselves for the challenges ahead.

This *Player's Handbook* is designed to either accompany *In His Grip*, or stand alone as a bible study. Together they will help you strengthen your foundation for both golf and life as you study on your own or in a small group. This foundation for life is firmly built upon the principles of Scripture and on a vital living relationship with Jesus Christ. That is what it means to be "In His Grip," experiencing a lifetime of learning and growing with God. It is never too late to begin building this solid foundation, and the teacher is ready.

THE MASTER TEACHER

Jesus taught in parables, stories about everyday life that held spiritual and eternal truths in them. Our goal is to do the same thing, specifically for golfers, using parallels between the game of golf and the game of life. This handbook and *In His Grip* will help you to make the application of God's principles and the teachings of Jesus to your own life.

Allow God to be your teacher through the Bible and your time of prayer with him. Seek to build a relationship with God and his Son Jesus through the time you spend with him. He wants you to spend time with him and to learn from him. Like learning golf from a pro, it is impossible to learn if you do not ask him to teach you and take the time to learn from his instruction. Unlike a busy golf pro, Jesus is not booked up in his lesson schedule. He is always available. Don't be afraid to be honest with him and to make the commitment it takes to learn from him.

TRAINING AIDS

Training aids help you recognize and follow the right swing path. The word of God is like a training aid for the course of life. The word of God is "living and active, sharper than any two-edged sword, . . . and discerning the thoughts and intentions of the heart" (Hebrews 4:12). God's word is a training aid of enormous value. In fact, it is your greatest training aid for life. This handbook will help you use the Bible as a training aid for your life.

WARMING UP

Dedicated golfers and athletes in all sports recognize the need to warm up before practicing or playing. Far too few of us are in the habit of warming up before a round of golf. Thus, we are not stretched out and limber, are more prone to injury, and do not play as well as we could otherwise.

Our spiritual life with Christ is the same way. We should warm up before heading out into the world of responsibility as a parent, spouse, employee, and friend to those around us. Our spiritual warm-up should include reading from God's word and reflecting on its application for our lives that day. Our spiritual warm-up includes prayer—praising God, asking His forgiveness, and seeking his help.

In His Grip and this handbook will help you warm up for the day. They will give you ideas to help you draw closer to God as your partner. You'll discover ways to walk with him each day. You will find wisdom for a more fulfilling life of faith in Jesus Christ. It has been said that a man stands the tallest on his knees before God each day. That is how we are to get ready to play the most difficult course of all . . . the course of life.

SWING THOUGHTS FOR THE DAY

Just as you should start each round of golf with a single principle or swing thought to be applied, so it is each day of life. *In His Grip* contains principles for life that need to be practiced if they are going to be learned and made useful. Those principles will not be formed into habits in a single day. Thus, you can reflect on them and the relevant Bible passages, with the intention of learning them over time. Jot down your own Swing Thought(s) that you want to apply from each devotion.

SHARING THE COMMITMENT

Golf is to be played and discussed with others. We like sharing our commitment to the game—encouraging one another, pointing out the strong points of a friend's game, enjoying the great shots and scenery together, and lamenting what went wrong on a certain hole or shot.

So it is with the application of the spiritual principles from the Bible. Just as Tom Lehman and Steve Jones talked about the Old Testament book of Joshua during their final round of the 1996 U. S. Open, you may want to talk about these ideas with a friend who shares your interest.

We hope you find a few others who want to study these foundations from *In His Grip* with you. The handbook will help you study together as it did for a group of PGA club professionals in Minneapolis who meet each week for a breakfast fellowship. It is also what several groups of amateur golfers use for their bible study in their town, church, or golf club. They have found that the lesson, scripture, and study questions generate good discussion and insights. Some groups combine it with golf lessons or time playing a round together.

JOURNAL OF IDEAS AND LESSONS

Harvey Penick is known for the wisdom and insights he recorded in his *Little Red Book*, originally a red notebook. You, too, can record insights and wisdom for your life and golf game as you read, discuss, and apply the thoughts in this book. By noting them in your own journal or log, they will be remembered. Like Mr. Penick, you may share these ideas with friends. You will be learning and helping others. This handbook gives you space to record these insights as you work through the foundations on your own or in a group.

LIVING IN HIS GRIP

The foundations are about the God who loves us so much that he gave his Son that we might live freely and eternally. God wants us to have a relationship with him. He wants us "in his grip" so that he can care for us and show us the truth he has revealed in the Bible. God gives us the choice of accepting or rejecting his grip. If we accept, he guides and protects us. His hands are like those of a father who shows his son how to hold the golf club, walks with his son in the fairway, and talks with his son about the game and life. Like our earthly father, Jesus cannot play the game for us. We must venture into a world full of bunkers and hazards . . . challenges and lessons to be learned. It is a life full of opportunity, joy to be shared with others, and rewards for those who remain faithful.

Challenge yourself and each other to make the commitment to live "In His Grip." Even if we fall short, we have assurance of God's comfort.

May God Keep You In His Grip!

Jim and *Wally*

In His Grip

The steps of a man are from the
LORD,
and he establishes him
in whose way he delights;

though he fall,
he shall not be cast headlong,
for the LORD
is the stay of his hand.

Psalms 37:23-24 KJV

ISBN 1-887002-95-2

Cross Training Publishing
P.O. Box 1541
Grand Island, NE 68802
(800) 430-8588

**Published in association with the literary agency of Alive Communications,
Inc., 1465 Kelly Johnson Blvd., Suite 320, Colorado Springs, Colorado, 80920.**

Scripture taken from the HOLY BIBLE: NEW INTERNATIONAL VER-
SION®. NIVR. COPYRIGHT© 1973, 1978, 1984, International Bible Society.
Used by permission of Zondervan Bible Publishers.

The NIV and New International Version trademarks are registered in the United
States Patent and Trademark Office by International Bible Society.

.

This book is manufactured in the United States of America.

Library of Congress Cataloging in Publication Data in Progress.

Published by Cross Training Publishing,
P.O. Box 1541
Grand Island, NE 68802
1-800-430-8588
Website: crosstrainingpub.com

SECTION 1

On the Tee

PART ONE

Living in God's Grip

KEY VERSE

If the LORD delights in a man's way, he makes his steps firm;
though he stumble, he will not fall, for the LORD upholds him with
his hand. (Psalm 37:23-24)

Personal Reflection and Discussion Questions

1. The Swing Thought identifies three things for which we should thank God. Why should we be thankful for each of these?
   (a) for his Son Jesus,
   (b) for his Word
   (c) for obstacles God puts in our path to help us learn.

2. Have you had an experience in which you noted a Bible passage and then later came back to your notes? What happened?

3. What does this mean—"If the LORD delights in a man's way, he makes his steps firm"? What is meant by:
   (a) man's way
   (b) he makes his steps firm
   (c) the Lord delights in

4. Have you ever experienced being "upheld by the Lord"? What happened and how did the Lord uphold you?

5. In what ways might we each fall and need to be upheld? Is there a way right now that you need to be upheld by the Lord and by those who care for you?

Additional Study *1 Samuel 2:1-10 (especially 9-10); Psalm 147:6,11*

Swing Thought

Thank God even for the obstacles in your path—those ever-present"bunkers."
They will help you learn patience and make
you aware of God's faithfulness.

KEY VERSE

"Have I not commanded you? Be strong and courageous. Do not be terrified; do not be discouraged, for the LORD your God will be with you wherever you go." (Joshua 1:9)

Personal Reflection and Discussion Questions

1. What do you think it means in these verses to "be strong"?

   What does it mean to "be courageous"?

2. When you read these verses in Joshua, are you reminded of times when you needed to be strong and courageous with the help of the Lord? What happened?

3. Do you have a friend who has, or who will, come alongside of you and give you encouragement and remind you of God's promises? If so, describe what it is that he/she has done.

4. For whom do you need to be the encourager? How can you come alongside of him/her and provide that support and encouragement?

5. God will make you alert to the needs of those around you. Where can God help you see and hear the needs of others he puts in your path?

Additional Study Deuteronomy 5:1-21, 32-33; 31:7-8, 23; Psalm 1:1-6

Swing Thought

Regardless what pressures and challenges you face today, remember that God knows your name. He cares about you and wants to give you his strength and courage. He also wants you to be an encouragement to others.

KEY VERSE

May the God of hope fill you with all joy and peace as you trust in him, so that you may overflow with hope by the power of the Holy Spirit. (Romans 15:13)

Personal Reflection and Discussion

1. What is the biggest "Hallelujah" experience you have ever had? When were you most excited and full of praise for what God had done?

2. Read Romans 15:5 out loud. Describe what each phrase means:
   (a) God of endurance and encouragement
   (b) a spirit of unity among yourselves
   (c) as you follow Christ Jesus
   (d) with one heart and mouth you may glorify the God and Father of our Lord Jesus Christ.

3. Do the same with verse 13. How should you relate to God and how will he relate to you?

4. Why can we "abound in hope" even when the circumstances of our lives do not seem all that hopeful? (See verse four for one thought.)

5. For what cause do we have this hope?

   What goal or goals are we striving to fulfill?

   Who is the source of that hope? (See verses 1-13.)
   (Also see Colossians 1:5, 23, 27; Hebrews 10:19-25.)

Additional Study *Colossians 1:5, 23, 27; Hebrews 10:19-25; Revelation 19:1-10 (Note the use of the word "Hallelujah.")*

Swing Thought

Hallelujah! To God be the glory for the courage, stability, and peace he gives us during our most difficult times.

KEY VERSE

I do not want to see you now and make only a passing visit; I hope to spend some time with you, if the Lord permits.
(I Corinthians 16:7)

Personal Reflection and Discussion Questions

1. How often do you consider or thank God for your victories?
   Are we responsible for our own efforts and results?

2. Describe how each title in italics summarizes the verse(s). How does each step apply to your life right now?

a. *First Priorities* (verses 4-5): Our key priorities must be consistent with God's priorities.

b. *Flexible Commitments* (verses 6-7): Our more detailed commitments, which may change . . . occur only "if the Lord permits."

c. *Faith in God's Provision* (verse 6): We can have faith that he will provide.

d. Adapt to the practical *Flow of Life* (verse 8): Be flexible because circumstances change. Our direction must change to adapt without compromising our priorities.

e. The result will be *Fruitful Fields* (verse 9): There will be open doors for effective work in bearing fruit for the Lord.

f. *Frustrating Foes* (verse 9): Adversaries will oppose the work of the Lord in your life. They will be frustrating.

3. How do you think the assembled members of the Royal Lytham & St. Anne's reacted to Tom Lehman's acceptance speech when he gave the credit to God for winning the 1996 British Open? What is your own reaction? What might you have said if you had just won the British Open?

Additional Study

Acts 18:20-21; II Thessalonians 3:5; II Peter 1:3-11

Swing Thought

Be on the lookout for fruitful fields in your life. At the same time, be aware of frustrating foes who might throw up roadblocks and try to keep you from being your best for God. Remember, he is at work in your life.

KEY VERSE

I can do everything through him who gives me strength.
(Philippians 4:13)

Personal Reflection and Discussion Questions

1. Do you have more discipline in your golf game or your faith?

   How could you increase your discipline and perseverance in each?

2. What does Paul mean in verse 11 when he writes that he has learned to be content whatever his state?

3. A paraphrase of verse 13 is "I can adjust to God's will for my life, whether it be good or bad, because he gives me the strength to do so." In what area of your life do you need the strength of the Lord in order to adjust to what is happening to you?

4. What is the secret of facing plenty or hunger, and abundance or want, as described by Paul in verse 12? (Also see Philippians 4:19.)

5. When have you felt like giving up, but persevered as Tom Lehman did when he considered leaving the tour? How do you know if you are to persevere or to give in and try a new direction for your life? (See John 15:1-8.)

Additional Study *James 1:3; Romans 15:4-6; I Corinthians 15:58; John 15:1-8*

Swing Thought

Today, ask God to keep you disciplined in your faith. And pray for his strength and power to help you persevere in all things.

KEY VERSE

. . . for the LORD will be your confidence . . . (Proverbs 3:26a)

Personal Reflection and Discussion Questions

1. Are you more likely to be over-confident or lacking in confidence?

   How would others describe your level of confidence?

2. How can you gain more confidence?

   What is God's role and what is your role?

   What does the passage in Proverbs say about this?

   Can we expect God to give us a quick fix of confidence?

3. Describe your view of the similarities and the differences between strength (be strong) and courage (be courageous) as they relate to building your confidence.

4. What does winning mean to you in your life?

   What do you want to "win" in order to find satisfaction in your life?

Additional Study

*Colossians 1:11; Ephesians 3:16; I Samuel 23:16; 30:6;
Philippians 4:13; Romans 16:25; II Corinthians 5:6-10*

Swing Thought

Winning in life requires a confidence that comes only from God—from understanding what he wants us to do and accepting his strength (ability) and his courage (willpower) to do it. The result? We become successful in what he sees as significant.

PART TWO

Purpose and Direction for Life

KEY VERSE

For the word of God is living and active. Sharper than any double-edged sword; it penetrates even to dividing soul and spirit, joints and marrow; it judges the thoughts and attitudes of the heart.
(Hebrews 4:12)

Personal Reflection and Discussion Questions

1. What does the following statement mean? "Success lies in what we do as a person." What are some measures or indicators of success?

   How does the statement on success contrast with this statement: "Significance lies in who we are as a person"?

   What are some measures or indicators of significance?

   How does Hebrews 4:11-12 apply to this?

2. Did the environment where you grew up tend to reward (a) what you did in life (success) or (b) who you were (significance)? Explain.

3. How can you help your children, or other young people, learn to achieve significance by who they are as a person (instead of by only focusing on what they do to succeed)?

4. How can you strive for significance as well as success in your golf?

5. How do you think God evaluates us when he looks down on us from heaven? What do you think will be important to him as he reviews your life on earth—your current life and your life in total?

Additional Study *James 1:1-27; I Peter 1:13-25; II Peter 1:3-10*
(Note: These passages are like formulas for significance.)

Swing Thought

Would you like to learn to evaluate yourself and others as God does? Ask him to help you concentrate on being rather than doing. Be assured that he will give you the strength and patience to know that as you do this, you are on the right track.

KEY VERSE

If any man builds on this foundation using gold, silver, costly stones, wood, hay or straw, his work will be shown for what it is, because the Day will bring it to light. It will be revealed with fire, and the fire will test the quality of each man's work.
(I Corinthians 3:12-13)

Personal Reflection and Discussion Questions

1. What do you want your "chapter" to include when people "read" about your accomplishments in life?

2. What are the "majors" that God has called you to "win" in your life? What does God see as significant in your life?

3. What can we achieve in life that will have eternal value? (See I Corinthians 3:10-15 for some ideas.)

4. What have you done in your life of eternal significance?

5. How did your view of what is important change as you reached 45 to 55 years of age? (or) How do you expect it will change as you approach that age?

Additional Study *Read II Corinthians 5:16-21*

Swing Thought

What are the "majors" that God has called you to "win" in your life? What do you want your "chapter" to include? Is there anything you prefer that the writer leave out?

. . . asking God to fill you with the knowledge of his will through all spiritual wisdom and understanding. (Colossians 1:9b)

Personal Reflection and Discussion Questions

1. Why do we learn so much about ourselves on the golf course?

2. In Colossians 1:9-14, Paul is praying to encourage us in our faith. What does each point mean? How does each apply to you?

   (a) be filled with the knowledge of God's will... and have spiritual wisdom and understanding

   (b) live a life worthy of the Lord and may please him in every way

   (c) bearing fruit

   (d) growing in the knowledge of God

   (e) being strengthened with all power according to his glorious might so that you may have great endurance and patience

   (f) joyfully giving thanks to the Father who has qualified you to share in the inheritance of the saints in the kingdom of light

   (g) recognize we have been rescued from the dominion of darkness and brought into the kingdom of the Son he loves

3. Only God can do each of these in, and through, you.
   Thank God for what he has revealed to you.
   How do you want him to further help you?

4. Summarize what these scriptures say about how we come to "know him" and "make him known."

Additional Study *Ephesians 1:15-23; 4:1; 3:16; 5:20; 6:12; Romans 12:1-2*
(Ways to have a life of learning.)

Swing Thought

Lord, on and off the golf course, give me the wisdom to learn more about myself as I focus on you. I pray that you will give me the strength I need to make it through the peaks and valleys as I become the person you created me to be.

KEY VERSE

But those who hope in the LORD will renew their strength. They will soar on wings like eagles; they will run and not grow weary, they will walk and not be faint. (Isaiah 40:31)

Personal Reflection and Discussion Questions

"Today's Preparation is tomorrow's performance" was the motto that Bobby Clampett claimed during the British Open in 1983.

1. In what ways has your physical or mental preparation paid off in performance at work, in golf, or in other situations?

2. When have you failed to be prepared mentally and physically? What were the results?

3. Beneath the surface, Bobby has something deeper in mind when he says, ". . . the longest lasting patience (and most significant performance) comes from having a well-defined purpose for existence, a reason for being and an ultimate goal in life." Bobby's "ultimate reason for being" and "ultimate goal in life" is focused on his relationship with Jesus Christ as Lord.

   What is your ultimate reason for being?

   What is your ultimate goal in life?

4. Preparation also includes spiritual preparation. How can we prepare spiritually for the demands of tomorrow?

5. What does Isaiah 40:28-31 tell us about the nature of spiritual preparation and the expected impact on our performance?

Additional Study *Psalms 119:25-32; 103:1-13; Genesis 35:1-4*

Swing Thought

It's God's promise to you: today's preparation and the renewing strength of your heavenly Father will give you the performance of an eagle for tomorrow.

KEY VERSE

We have different gifts, according to the grace given us. If a man's gift is prophesying, let him use it in proportion to his faith.
(Romans 12:6)

Personal Reflection and Discussion Questions

1. What does Romans 12:1-2 mean to you (phrase by phrase)?

2. What have you discovered about your uniqueness for service in God's kingdom?

   How are you uniquely designed, talented, and gifted?

3. What are some of the special ways God has utilized you?

   How does he utilize your unique design as a person?

4. What is your dream or vision of how you want God to use you in the future? In other words, as you "find your game" in God's kingdom, what do you hope and pray it will involve and look like?

5. Has "finding your game" involved any of the gifts of the Holy Spirit in Romans 12:3-8, I Corinthians 12:8-10, 28, and Ephesians 4:11?

Additional Study *I Corinthians 12:8-10, 28; Ephesians 4:11*

Swing Thought

In golf, to "find your game" means to learn to play the best you can within your unique set of capabilities and with the most complementary equipment. In life it means to find out how God has uniquely designed and gifted you for service in his kingdom.

PART THREE

Preparation for the Course

KEY VERSE

. . . your teachers will be hidden no more; with your own eyes you will see them. Whether you turn to the right or to the left, your ears will hear a voice behind you, saying, "This is the way; walk in it."
(Isaiah 30:20b-21)

Personal Reflection and Discussion Questions

1. Have you ever had a serious problem with your golf swing and elected to go to a teacher or friend for help?

   Was that person gracious to the sound of your cry for help?

   How did they show, or fail to show, graciousness?

2. Why (and how) do you trust your golf instructor?

3. How do we know God will be gracious to our cry for help? (See verses 18-22.)

   Have you experienced His graciousness? Describe the situation.

4. What does it mean to trust God for his wisdom and direction in life?

5. Why do we need to spend time with God to get to know and trust him?

   How can we spend time with him?

   How can we spend more time with him even though our day is busy?

Additional Study *1 Corinthians 12:8-10, 28; Ephesians 4:11*

Swing Thought

Learning to trust a golf instructor is like learning to trust God for his instruction. If you mess around without lessons for too long, the game of your life will show the results. But once you get the help you need, it's a different story. Are you ready to start working with the Pro for your life?

KEY VERSE

*"But you are not to be called 'Rabbi,' for you have only one Master
(. . . the Christ . . .) and you are all brothers."
(Matthew 23:8,10)*

Personal Reflection and Discussion Questions

1. Why do you think only 8% of the golfers have had a lesson from an instructor?

   Have you had a lesson or lessons? Why or why not?

2. What should you look for in a golf instructor?

3. Which of those same characteristics would you look for in a teacher about faith (i.e. a bible study leader or a pastor)?

   What additional characteristics would you expect?

4. What characteristics does Jesus have that make him the best teacher?

5. What are the responsibilities of the student learning to play golf?

   What are the responsibilities of the student in learning about faith?

Additional Study *John 14:25-31; 1:35-42; 3:1-6; Luke 12:11-12*

Swing Thought

*There is no other teacher like the Trinity of God the Father, the Son, and
the Holy Spirit. Each, in his own way, is there to guide, instruct,
and correct the "swings" of your life.*

KEY VERSE

So then, just as you received Christ Jesus as Lord, continue to live in him, rooted and built up in him, strengthened in the faith as you were taught . . . (Colossians 2:6-7)

Personal Reflection and Discussion Questions

1. Psalm 103:1-13 offers about 15 different benefits of the Lord. List them in brief two-or three-word phrases. (It is easier to form good godly habits when we know that he offers all of these benefits.)

2. Which of those good godly habits has been the hardest for you to develop and why?

3. How does God help us in our habit formation? Especially note about three things in Colossians 2:6-7 that help us form good habits. Describe what they mean.

4. How can you continue to work on improving these habits?

5. What other points were particularly helpful or meaningful in the additional study verses?

Additional Study *Psalm 103:1-13; I Thessalonians 4:1-8; Ephesians 2:19-22; Galatians 2:20*

Swing Thought

Habit formation in golf and the renewing of our mind in Christ are both enhanced by solid teaching, devotion, commitment, and the encouragement of others. Make sure all these components are part of your game of golf, and your game of life.

KEY VERSE

May the words of my mouth and the meditation of my heart be pleasing in your sight, O LORD, my Rock and my Redeemer.
(Psalm 19:14)

Personal Reflection and Discussion Questions

1. What is the meaning of each of these phrases in Psalm 19:7-11? Journal your thoughts to see what you learn.

Form of God's Direction	Quality of the Direction for Us	What It Does
The law ....of the Lord	...is perfect.	Revives the soul.
The testimony.......... "	...is sure.	Makes wise the simple.
The precepts........... "	...are right.	Rejoices the heart.
The commandment.. "	...is pure.	Enlightens the eyes.
The fear ....…..... "	...is clean.	Endures forever.
The ordinances ...... "	...are true and righteous.	
	...are more to be desired than gold (or golf).	
	...are sweeter also than honey.	
By them	...thy servant is warned.	
In keeping them	...there is great reward.	

2. Do you take notes on the sermon and review them, mark passages in your Bible, keep track of prayers, or track significant events in your life? What would be the advantages? How could you keep it simple but useful?

3. Information about your game and practice time clarifies strengths and limitations and helps you practice more systematically. What information would be most helpful for you to record about your golf game? (Wally has some golf logs that can help.)

Additional Study *Psalms 19:7-11; 104:33-34 (desire to please him); 119:33-40 (desire to learn God's truth and direction), 137-144 (the merits of God's direction/path).*

Swing Thought

Tap into the treasure of your own experience with a journal for your golf game and for your time with God. You'll not only see your daily progress, but you'll also see how God speaks to you in special ways. Your journal will become the most valued book in your entire library. Today would be a good day to make your first entry.

KEY VERSE

I have hidden your word in my heart that I might not sin against you. (Psalm 119:11)

Personal Reflection and Discussion Questions

1. Have you ever used a training aid to help you learn some aspect of the golf swing or putting stroke? What was the device and how was it designed to help you?

   Did it help? Why or why not?

2. How is this study guide a training aid for the Bible and your life?

   Is it helping? Why or why not?

   In what ways does the group contribute to the value of the training aid?

3. In what way is scripture a training aid for life?
   — (See II Timothy 3:16-17.)

4. Why is the Bible the single most important training aid for life as a Christian?

5. What are some other training aids for strengthening your knowledge of God and your relationship with Christ?

   Are they helpful? (Our CD with the song "In His Grip" is an example of a spiritual training aid.)

Additional Study *II Timothy 3:10-17; I Timothy 6:3-16*

Swing Thought

Training aids for both our golf game and for our walk with Christ must be carefully selected and suited to our needs. Just as there are people who want to sell you a "bill of goods," so there will be ideas and ideologies that will not be an aid to your spiritual growth. That's why the Bible encourages us to be wise as serpents, but harmless as doves. The key word must always be discernment.

KEY VERSE

Hear, O Israel: The LORD our God, the LORD is one. Love the LORD your God with all your heart and with all your soul and with all your strength. These commandments that I give you today are to be upon your hearts. (Deuteronomy 6:5-6)

Personal Reflection and Discussion Questions

1. Describe the parallel between "live hands" in the golf swing and a "loving heart" in life.

2. How can you develop a "loving heart" toward God and other people? What is your role and the role of God?

3. The passages in Deuteronomy 6:4-5 and Mark 12:28-31 (also Luke 10:27) are the Great Commandment. What does it really mean? (Note: Jesus added "mind" to the other three because in Hebrew thinking the heart was considered the seat of intelligence.)

4. How would you live and behave differently if you took very seriously the Great Commandment?

5. Likewise, how would it change your life if you took very seriously the second commandment to "Love your neighbor as yourself"?

Additional Study *Deuteronomy 4:29-31; Ezekiel 11:19-21; I John 4:7-21; II Thessalonians. 3:5; John 7:37-39; Psalms 119:10-11; 108:1-5*

Swing Thought

Developing "live hands" takes practice and usually the help of a golf professional. In the same way, God will give you his own loving heart when you humble yourself in his holy presence.

Search me, O God, and know my heart; test me and know my anxious thoughts. (Psalm 139:23)

Personal Reflection and Discussion Questions

1. What does the term "swing thought" mean to you?

   What are some swing thoughts for golf that you or others have used?

2. Why do we use swing thoughts? How can we misuse them?

3. What "swing thoughts" do you have for your life? (They might be from this or another study, books, training, etc.)

   Where do you (can you) write down your swing thoughts?

4. Some swing thoughts can come from the Bible, Christian music, or Christian literature. They may be the titles of some of the lessons in this study. Which lesson title would you use as a swing thought for your life?

5. What are other good swing thoughts for you today?

Additional Study *Philippians 4:4-9; Psalms 26:1-7; 5:1-3; Proverbs 15:9*

Swing Thought

This might be a good time to create two or three swing thoughts of your own.

KEY VERSE

Dishonest money dwindles away, but he who gathers money little by little makes it grow. (Proverbs 13:11)

Personal Reflection and Discussion Questions

1. What percent of your golf shots are from within 60 yards of the hole?

   Why don't you and others learn to improve your short game?

   What could you easily do to work on your own short game? How could you "gather" the skills and habits "little by little"?

2. Name areas of your life where improvement comes in little increments.

3. Why does the verse say "dishonest money dwindles away"? How does that fit with your experience and observations of others?

4. Proverbs 14:23 says, "All hard work brings a profit, but mere talk leads only to poverty." What does that say about your golf game?

   What are some areas of life you want to improve or achieve?

5. List the little ways you can make a big difference from Romans 12:9- 21. (Look for one in each verse.)

Additional Study *Proverbs 14:23; Romans 12:9-21*

Swing Thought

It's the many little things each day that occur in life that reveal the presence of God. They need practice just like the short shots in golf.

KEY VERSE

I meditate on your precepts and consider your ways.
(Psalm 119:15)

Personal Reflection and Discussion Questions

1. Watch the pre-shot routine of some of your golfing friends and tour pros. Also carefully review your own pre-shot routine. Perhaps videotape yourself and others.

   What is the purpose of the pre-shot routine?

   Is it fulfilling its purpose in your golf game?

2. What is your "pre-shot routine" for starting out your day?

   Do you prepare properly mentally, emotionally, physically, and spiritually? Why or why not?

3. What can you do to establish better habits of prayer, reading God's word, and reflection on God in a quiet time with him?

4. How can we encourage each other to develop the discipline of a regular time with God?

5. Some people use the ACTS acrostic to remind them to include these four areas in their prayer. ACTS—Adoration, Confession, Thanksgiving, and Supplication. Discuss what is included in each.

Additional Study
Psalms 119:23, 48, 78; 46:10; 47:1-9; Matthew 6:5-14; I Thessalonians 5:16-18

Swing Thought

How can you modify and practice your "pre-shot" and "pre-day" routines to make them more helpful and meaningful? A good idea may be to take out a piece of paper and jot down a few things you would like from your daily time with God. Right now would be a great time to start.

Prayer Requests & Notes

SECTION 2

On the Fairway

PART FOUR

Fundamentals for Golf
and Life

KEY VERSE

All Scripture is God-breathed and is useful for teaching, rebuking, correcting and training in righteousness, so that the man of God may be thoroughly equipped for every good work.
(II Timothy 3:16-17)

Personal Reflection and Discussion Questions

1. Why is the grip, the placement of the hands on the club, regarded by most instructors as the fundamental factor in the golf swing?

2. Why is having a "grip on the word of God" probably the most important fundamental for living a godly life?

   What do the verses for this lesson say about that? (Notice II Timothy 2:14-15 and II Timothy 3:14-15.)

3. What does the phrase "all Scripture is God-breathed" mean?

4. What does II Timothy 3:16 say are the four purposes of the Scriptures? What does each mean?

5. What does II Timothy 3:17 say Scripture is designed to do?

   Are you close to, or far from, being "complete, equipped for every good work"? Why?

Additional Study Romans 15:4; Psalm 19:7-14; Hebrews 5:11-14; Deuteronomy 4:1, 10; 11:18-25

Swing Thought

Gripping the golf club properly is the key to effective golfing. Gripping God's Word is the key to effective living—a life of joy and significance.

KEY VERSE

*But the seed on good soil stands for those with a noble and good heart,
who hear the word, retain it, and by persevering produce a crop.*
(Luke 8:15)

Personal Reflection and Discussion Questions

1. What is the word of God compared to in Luke 8:9-15?

   Why is this a good comparison?

2. What are the four types of soil on which the seed can fall?

   How do they compare to four categories of people who might hear
   the word of God?

   What are the three things which can prevent the word from having
   its full effect in your life...and producing fruit?

3. What were the characteristics of the good soil?

   How can you be more like the good soil?

4. To have a feel for the golf grip you must take hold of a club.
   However, the grip is so subtle that even experienced players need to
   check it. Describe the parallels between these two ideas: the need to
   take a hold of, read, and apply the word of God and the need to have
   a live-handed grip on a golf club.

Additional Study *James 1:22-25; Mark 4:13-20; Matthew 13:3-9*

Swing Thought

*Take hold of God's Word in your hand, hear it with your mind, and hold it
fast in your heart. You do not need to understand it all. God will give you
the understanding you need.*

KEY VERSE

This is how we know what love is: Jesus Christ laid down his life for us. And we ought to lay down our lives for our brothers.
(I John 3:16)

Personal Reflection and Discussion Questions

1. One demonstration of true commitment and love was that Jesus gave his own life for us. Describe what that means for you.

2. What have you done lately that demonstrated your "love" for another person other than a family member? (It need not be a grand event. It could be a simple act of kindness to another person, even someone you did not know.)

   What was your source of motivation or inspiration?

3. What does I John 3:16 mean when it says that "we ought to lay down our lives for our brothers"?

4. What evidence is there besides Jesus' death on the cross that God loves us and wants us to love him and others in return?

5. The "drill" for developing a "loving heart" is to allow God to change your heart so you become more like him. Pray—asking God to do this in your life.

   What will you do to be more like him today?

Additional Study *I John 4:19-21; Romans 12:9-10; Matthew 20:25-28; I Corinthians 10:24; Hebrews 13:1-2; Ephesians 5:1-2; Galatians 5:13-15*

Swing Thought

If you will only ask him, God will give you a loving heart for himself and others. The only drill required is your complete trust in him.

KEY VERSE

. . . stand firm. Let nothing move you. Always give yourselves fully to the work of the Lord, because you know that your labor in the Lord is not in vain. (I Corinthians 15:58)

Personal Reflection and Discussion Questions

1. Why is a steadfast position so important in the golf swing?

   Describe this parallel between golf and life in your own words.

2. What does it mean to "stand firm. Let nothing move you. Always give yourselves fully to the work of the Lord"?

3. In what ways would you like to be more like that description?

4. Do you tend to be overly optimistic, overly pessimistic, or balanced and realistic most of the time?

   How can you move toward being more realistic and balanced?

5. What does it mean to say that the "labor is not in vain"? Does it mean the labor has good results, or something else?

6. How can we know that "in the Lord our labor is not in vain"? (Especially note the Additional Study Section.)

Additional Study *II Corinthians 4:7-12, 16-18; Hebrews 10:19-25; I Peter 5:10-11*

Swing Thought

Your labor will never be in vain if you remain steadfast and immovable in your position with the Lord.

KEY VERSE

. . . asking God to fill you with the knowledge of his will through all spiritual wisdom and understanding. And we pray this in order that you may live a life worthy of the Lord and may please him in every way: bearing fruit in every good work, growing in the knowledge of God. (Colossians 1:9b-10)

Personal Reflection and Discussion Questions

1. How would you describe the concept of alignment in golf and in life?

   What is it that we want to be aligned with in our golf swings?

   What is it that we want to be aligned with in our lives?

2. How easy is it to get off alignment in golf? In life, what other kinds of things may we knowingly or unknowingly become aligned with?

3. When we are properly aligned in life, we will have the kind of results which Paul describes in Colossians 1:9-13. List those results and describe what they mean.

4. This passage is called the Apostolic prayer because Paul prayed it for the people. We can also pray this prayer for ourselves and for those that we want to encourage in the Lord. Pray this prayer for yourself— to be aligned, to grow in wisdom and knowledge, and to bear fruit.

   List others for whom you will pray this prayer.

Additional Study *Colossians 1:3-8; Ephesians 1:15-23; 4:1-7; Romans 12:1-2*

Swing Thought

Place an imaginary club on the ground and point it directly at Jesus Christ. As you do this, what do you feel he expects of you? In what ways do you need to adjust your alignment? What must you do to focus more intently on him? What will you need to do to stay on alignment?

KEY VERSE

*... how God anointed Jesus of Nazareth with the Holy Spirit
and power ... (Acts 10:38a)*

Personal Reflection and Discussion Questions

1. What are the primary sources of power in the golf swing?

   What is the relative importance of each of these sources of power?

2. What are the various categories of power available in our bodies and minds as we pursue other tasks?

3. The Holy Spirit is at work in the life of every believer. What is the basic role of the power of the Holy Spirit in the life of a believer? (See references Acts 1:8, Romans 8:16, Luke 12:12, John 6:23, Ephesians 4:30, John 16:7,8, John 3:5, I Corinthians 2:12, Romans 8:11, 26, along with those in the Additional Study section.)

4. How does the power of the Holy Spirit manifest itself in the life of a believer? (Be aware that there may be differences in beliefs regarding the power and evidence of the Holy Spirit in this time frame. If you are sensitive to others and not dogmatic in your views, everyone will learn more.)

5. What are the unique roles of the Father, Son, and Holy Spirit in our lives?

Additional Study John 14:25-31; 15:15-17; 16:7-15; Ephesians 1:19-23; 3:20; Romans 15:13

Swing Thought

Are you fully aware of the power source that God has given you? Don't fail to understand and rely on the power of the Holy Spirit at work in your life. This would be a good day to re-evaluate your understanding of this, and to begin tapping God's power as never before.

KEY VERSE

Do not conform any longer to the pattern of this world, but be transformed by the renewing of your mind. Then you will be able to test and approve what God's will is—his good, pleasing and perfect will.
(Romans 12:2)

Personal Reflection and Discussion Questions

1. How is toning our physical muscles for golf something like toning our heart to serve God and other people?

2. We can exercise and make our spiritual heart more loving in two ways. First, we can exercise it by using it. Secondly, reading and meditating on God's Word will sensitize our spiritual heart. How can you be more loving of God and others?

3. In Romans 12:1-2, we see that Paul is encouraging us to do three things. How would you describe each of these three?

   (a) surrender to God (do not be conformed) by presenting our bodies as a living sacrifice (I Peter 2:1-10)

   (b) separate ourselves (be transformed) from the tendency to be conformed to the sinful ways around us (I Peter 1:17-21)

   (c) spiritually renew our minds (renewal of your mind) by a transformation (I Peter 1:13-16)

4. What habits or practices can you use to build muscle tone for golf?

5. What changes in your life will you make to better tone your heart/spiritual muscle? (See Additional Study for ideas.)

Additional Study *I Peter 1:13-21; 2:1-10; Ephesians 4:17-24; I John 2:15*

Swing Thought

A club in your hand and the use of it will tone your live-handed muscles. A Bible in your hand and the application of its message of love in your life will tone your loving-heart muscles.

PART FIVE

Unleashing Power: The Swing

KEY VERSE

Reaching into his bag and taking out a stone, he slung it and struck the Philistine on the forehead. The stone sank into his forehead, and he fell facedown on the ground. (I Samuel 17:49)

Personal Reflection and Discussion Questions

1. What insights about the story of David and Goliath do you have now that you may not have had before?

2. How did David employ the power of centrifugal force?

3. Describe the power of centrifugal force as it applies to the golf swing. What can golfers do to get the full power of centrifugal force in the swing?

4. What does it mean to say that believers in Christ have been given a "resurrection power" to live and serve in God's kingdom?

5. Why do we not always "succeed" as well as David did against Goliath?

   (a) In the life challenges we face?

   (b) In golf?

Additional Study *Philippians 3:10; Ephesians 1:10-23; 3:20-21; Acts 1:8; II Peter 1:3-4*

Swing Thought

God gives us much more than the centrifugal force of a slingshot or a golf club when he works in our lives. He gives us the God-sized power of his Holy Spirit, along with the courage, power, and wisdom to slay the "giants" in our lives. Remember, the battle belongs to the Lord.

KEY VERSE

For my yoke is easy, and my burden is light.
(Matthew 11:30)

Personal Reflection and Discussion Questions

1. How does it help golfers, and especially beginners, to "Be at Ease"?

2. In what way does the verse from Matthew 11:30 convey this same thought as it applies to our spiritual life with God?

3. In what ways is it true that Jesus' "yoke is easy" and his "burden is light"?

   How do we cause his yoke to be "hard" and his burden "heavy"?

4. How can you use your pre-shot routine to relax your muscles and ease your mind before hitting a shot?

5. How could you use a time of prayer and reflection on God each day as a "pre-shot" routine to prepare your mind and spirit for your day?

Additional Study Romans 8:1-11; Psalm 55:22; Colossians 3:2; Proverbs 14:30; John 14:1; 8:31-32

Swing Thought

Your long checklists for golf and life can be replaced with this simple guideline: Relax. Be at Ease!

KEY VERSE

Now the Lord is the Spirit, and where the Spirit of the Lord is, there is freedom. (II Corinthians 3:17)

Personal Reflection and Discussion Questions

1. Do you experience more tension than you should in your hands, arms, or body as you execute a golf shot? Why or why not?

2. Do you tend to impose worry and tension on yourself in most things you do in life? How? Why?

3. What is the nature of the "freedom" in II Corinthians 3:17?

   What does this mean: "where the Spirit of the Lord is . . ."?

4. While we have freedom, we also have responsibilities. What are our responsibilities in our relationship with God?

5. What do these phrases from verse 18 mean?

   (a) . . . with unveiled face

   (b) . . . beholding the glory of God

   (c) . . . being changed into his likeness from one degree of glory to another

   (d) . . . for this comes from the Lord who is the Spirit

Additional Study Galatians 2:4; 5:1, 13; Psalm 119:133

Swing Thought

God wants to give you freedom from the worry and tension of life. All you need to do is to listen to the Instructor.

KEY VERSE

"I tell you the truth, anyone who has faith in me will do what I have been doing. He will do even greater things than these, because I am going to the Father."
(John 14:12)

Personal Reflection and Discussion Questions

1. What does it mean to "trust our golf swing"?

2. What does it mean to "trust God in your life"?

3. What are the benefits of being tension-free in golf? . . . in your life?

4. What are the big issues for which you need to learn to trust God?

5. How can we learn to trust God in the big and difficult areas of life?

God truly loves us and wants us to love and to trust him. How does that help?

Additional Study *Psalms 40:4; 112:1-10; Jeremiah 17:7-8; Proverbs 3:5; 16:1-11, 20*

Swing Thought

Trust the Lord for the "shots" you face in your life today. He promises to direct your swing.

KEY VERSE

*Then we will no longer be infants, tossed back and forth by the waves,
and blown here and there by every wind of teaching and by the
cunning and craftiness of men in their deceitful scheming.
(Ephesians 4:14)*

Personal Reflection and Discussion Questions

1. Balance in the golf swing is very important, but hard to achieve. What causes us to be out of balance?

   What can we do to stay in balance in the golf swing?

2. An individual needs to have balance in his/her spiritual journey. How does Ephesians 4:14 describe balance for an individual?

3. In a group, team, or in the body of Christ, balance is achieved by abilities and gifts being distributed among the group. What different gifts are listed in Ephesians 4:9-16?

4. From verses 12-14, identify at least four reasons these gifts are given to people in the body.

5. Describe how the body, a group of believers, or any well-functioning team effort, functions together according to verses 15 and 16.

Additional Study James 1:5-8; Ephesians 1:15-23; 6:10-20 (armor); Psalm 119:125 (The gifts of the Holy Spirit are reviewed on page 118 of In His Grip.)

Swing Thought

Take the right stance, and God will give you the balance to release your full potential. He will do this today and every day of your life.

KEY VERSE

Those who live according to the sinful nature have their minds set on what that nature desires; but those who live in accordance with the Spirit have their minds set on what the Spirit desires.
(Romans 8:5)

Personal Reflection and Discussion Questions

1. E. M. Prain's definition of timing, and his description of how outstanding players hit the ball, provide some insight into the importance of timing. What are some of the common remedies golfers have for improving the timing of their golf swing?

2. The hands set the timing since they are the only part of the body in contact with the club. In what way is the Holy Spirit a similar control mechanism in our spiritual life? (Consider Romans 8:1-11 and I Corinthians 2:6-16.)

   How does the Holy Spirit serve as a control mechanism?

   How does the Holy Spirit influence the direction and timing of events in our lives?

   How do we allow the Holy Spirit to direct our lives?

   How can we drift away from the proper influence of the Holy Spirit?

3. Describe Romans 8:5-7 in your own words.

Additional Study *Romans 8:1-11 and I Corinthians 2:2-16.*

Swing Thought

Only when you allow the Holy Spirit to guide and direct your life will you have the "timing" you need to become the person God has designed you to be.

KEY VERSE

Trust in the LORD with all your heart and lean not on your own understanding; in all your ways acknowledge him, and he will make your paths straight. (Proverbs 3:5-6)

Personal Reflection and Discussion Questions

1. In the movie *Tin Cup*, golf pro Roy McAvoy (Kevin Costner) says, "That's what the golf swing is all about. It's about gaining control of your life and letting go at the same time." What does this mean to you?

2. Read the "Swing Thought." How can you let go and feel (experience) the freedom and power available in your golf swing?

   How can a person let go and know, or experience, the freedom and power available to us from God?

3. Read and reflect on Proverbs 3:5-12. Ask God to show you the meaning for you at this point in life. What does it mean to you?

4. Read and reflect on Psalm 37:3-7, especially note the meaning of:
   (a) trust in the Lord

   (b) delight yourself in the Lord

   (c) commit your way to the Lord

   (d) be still before the Lord

Additional Study *Spend time in Proverbs 3:1-12 and Psalm 37:3-7*

Swing Thought

The full, natural release of your life to God, like the release of your swing in golf, can only be achieved by letting go, and allowing yourself to feel (experience) the freedom and power so readily available. The power is there. It just needs to be recognized and tapped.

KEY VERSE

"On the contrary, we speak as men approved by God to be entrusted with the gospel. We are not trying to please men but God, who tests our hearts." (I Thessalonians 2:4)

Personal Reflection and Discussion Questions

1. What does a "gallery finish" mean?

2. Describe or videotape the follow through (finish) of your golf swing.

   How could you improve it?

3. How does this phrase apply to you? "On the contrary, we speak . . . not trying to please men, but God, who tests our hearts."

   (a) In what ways are you tempted to say or do what others want, even when you know it to be wrong?

   (b) What are the many ways in which our society causes us to want to please others with our speech and actions?

   (c) Why is this especially difficult for young people growing up today?

4. Who are the people in the "gallery" of your life who are most important to you?

   In what ways do you want them to respect and admire you?

   Why is seeking their flattery and affection an improper motive?

Additional Study *Acts 20:24-38; Galatians 1:10; II Corinthians 4:5-6*

Swing Thought

Throughout today, focus on God's expectations for you, not on the flattery and high hopes of people in the gallery of your life.

Prayer Requests & Notes

Help for the Hazards

PART SIX

Facing Adversity

KEY VERSE

But Jesus immediately said to them: "Take courage! It is I. Don't be afraid." (Matthew 14:27)

Personal Reflection and Discussion Questions

1. Why is adversity at the very essence of the game of golf?

   What are examples of adversity in golf?

2. How do these two concepts apply in golf?

   (a) anticipation to avoid adversity

   (b) practice for recovery from adversity

3. How can you avoid and recover from adversity you face in life?

4. How does God help you . . .

   (a) anticipate enough to avoid adversity?

   (b) practice for recovery from adversity?

5. What are some scripture verses that relate to the . . .

   (a) avoidance of adversity?

   (b) recovery from adversity?

Additional Study II Corinthians 6:1-10; I Thessalonians 3:1-10; Psalm 34:19-22

Swing Thought

If you are facing adversity today, ask Jesus Christ to come and calm the waves and the winds of your troubles. He promises to stick closer to you than a brother. Take him up on his generous promise.

KEY VERSE

But when he saw the wind, he was afraid and, beginning to sink, cried out, "Lord, save me!" (Matthew 14:30)

Personal Reflection and Discussion Questions

1. This devotional idea, and the one before it, came from a sermon by Pastor Larry Tindall of Bethel Church in Owatonna, Minnesota. What examples in your life relate to Pastor Larry's concept that we need to focus on the target instead of the adversity?

2. Based on Psalm 37:1-11, how will you view adversity and trials if you are committed, delighted, and trusting in the Lord?

   Do you do this? In what circumstances or situations?

3. The "target" of our lives should be our relationship with Christ. When we focus on him and trust him for our needs, there should be no need to worry about the circumstances. This is one result of abiding in Christ. Read Psalm 37:5-6. How can we focus on Jesus as the target and be less concerned about the adversity of our circumstances?

4. What adversity do you face in your life at this time? How would you like others to pray for these situations?

Additional Study Psalm 37:1-11; II Corinthians 4:16-18; Philippians 3:7-16

Swing Thought

Today, pay special attention to keeping your eyes and mind focused on Jesus. Your loving heavenly Father promises to give you his guidance and direction.

KEY VERSE

Blessed is the man who perseveres under trial, because when he has stood the test, he will receive the crown of life that God has promised to those who love him. (James 1:12)

Personal Reflection and Discussion Questions

1. What are the most challenging "bunkers of life" you have faced?

   What is your most current challenge or bunker?

   What have you learned, or what are you learning, from these bunkers?

2. Review Psalm 37:1-11 from the prior study. What does this passage tell us about how we are to handle these "bunkers of life" when we find ourselves in the middle of them?

3. Bunkers are opportunities to learn about God and to learn to trust him. In *The Way of Agape* Study Guide by Chuck & Nancy Missler (published by Koininia House), they say "The question is, 'Do you love (agapao) God enough that you are willing to die to your own justified hurts, fears, doubts, etc. so that His life can come forth through you?'" (John 21:15-17; Matthew 10:37-39; Luke 14:26-33)

   What is your response to their question? Why or why not?

4. How does your response in question #3 apply to your current "bunkers of life"?

5. Can you trust God to help you through whatever bunker(s) you may face today? How?

Additional Study
John 21:15-17; Matthew 10:37-39; Luke 14:26-33; Review Psalm 37:1-11.

Swing Thought

So you're in one of life's "bunkers" today? You hit it in there; now hit it out!

KEY VERSE

"But blessed is the man who trusts in the LORD, whose confidence is in him. He will be like a tree planted by the water that sends out its roots by the stream . . ." (Jeremiah 17:7-8a)

Personal Reflection and Discussion Questions

1. A "bad lie" in golf is when the ball is sitting in such a way that it is difficult to hit properly. Describe some of the worst golf lies you recall.

2. A "bad lie" in life is a difficult situation you must face, "hit" from, and then move on. What examples are you facing now?

3. So-called "winter" rules allow you to "bump" your ball to a better lie in your fairway. In life, we seldom get a "bump" to a "better lie." Instead we have to "play it as it lies." We must face the situation head on, hit our best shot, and then move on. Describe situations where you have successfully done this in your life.

4. When we learn to trust in the Lord, we are better able to face and deal with these "bad lies" in life. Contrast "trusting in man" (other people) verses "trusting in the Lord" as seen in Jeremiah 17:5-8.

5. Why is a tree planted by the stream so healthy?

   What do the stream and the water represent in this analogy?

   How are we to be like a tree planted by a stream?

Additional Study *Hebrews 10:30-39; Psalm 1:1-6; James 1:2-3*

Swing Thought

Trust God to give you the ability (provision) to play out of any difficult "lie" that comes your way. He will hear your prayer and give you the courage you need to play on.

KEY VERSE

The Lord disciplines those he loves, and he punishes everyone he accepts as a son. (Hebrews 12:6)

Personal Reflection and Discussion Questions

1. How do the hazards of the golf course discipline us to play better?

   How do designers build this into course designs?

2. What do we learn about the discipline of the Lord in Hebrews 12:3-11?

   Who does he discipline? Why?

3. What is the ultimate goal of the discipline we receive from the Lord?

4. What is the meaning of verse 11?

5. Describe an example of this discipline from the Lord in your life.

   What happened?

   How did you grow from it?

   How do you know it was discipline from the Lord?

Additional Study Deuteronomy 8:1-10; Psalm 94:12-15; Proverbs 3:11-12

Swing Thought

Discipline, like the hazards of the course, is placed strategically in our path as a reflection of God's desire for us to grow in his wisdom and love.

PART SEVEN

Prayer and Praise to God

KEY VERSE

You are worthy, our Lord and God, to receive glory and honor and power, for you created all things, and by your will they were created and have their being. (Revelation 4:11)

Personal Reflection and Discussion Questions

1. Why is God the ultimate course designer?

   Why do human course designers only operate within the boundaries of what God has created?

2. Describe some golf holes or courses where the designer has transformed a beautiful piece of nature "into a place where people who love to play golf are challenged to try their skills."

3. Discuss your reactions, thoughts, and feelings in response to a careful reading of Revelation 4:11.

4. Are you ever reminded of the awesome power and creativity of God while you are playing golf in the nature that he has created? Describe an experience, and discuss your thoughts and feelings about it.

5. Are you ever in awe of how God created you and other human beings in all our complexity and uniqueness? In what situations?

   Praise and thank him for how he has created us.

Additional Study *Genesis 1:1-13; Isaiah 40:28; 42:5-9; 45:18-19; Colossians 1:15-20; Psalm 148:1-14*

Swing Thought

Message to the greatest Designer of all: "Worthy art thou, our Lord and God, to receive glory and honor and power."

KEY VERSE

Let us fix our eyes on Jesus, the author and perfecter of our faith . . .
(Hebrews 12:2)

Personal Reflection and Discussion Questions

1. Why is alignment so important in the golf swing and in putting?

2. Why do we need to continue to look to Jesus as " . . . the author and perfecter of our faith . . ."?

3. When you strayed from proper spiritual alignment (eyes and mind aligned with Jesus), how were you reminded that you were out of alignment?

   How did you get realigned?

4. How does the discipline discussed in an earlier lesson tend to help our faith become "perfected"?

5. How do these sources help us stay aligned with Jesus?

   (a) God's word in the Bible

   (b) the guidance of the Holy Spirit

   (c) encouragement of friends who share our faith in Christ

Additional Study *Proverbs 3:13-20; Philippians 2:1-11; Hebrews 1:1-4*

Swing Thought

Jesus wants you to position yourself so that he can reflect his love, grace, and direction for your life. All it takes is a "mirror" in which you will be able to see his face.

KEY VERSE

Be joyful in hope, patient in affliction, faithful in prayer.
(Romans 12:12)

Personal Reflection and Discussion Questions

1. Describe how you would feel if you were playing in the final group of a major golf championship. What is your closest personal experience to this situation?

2. What is the meaning of each of these phrases?
   (a) rejoice in your hope

   (b) be patient in tribulation

   (c) be constant in prayer

3. Share with others the things for which you are currently
   (a) rejoicing and/or hoping.

   (b) patient, or trying to be patient.

   (c) praying earnestly.

4. How can we possibly pray constantly and get anything else accomplished?

5. What is the biggest challenge in your life today? How would you like others to pray for you over the next few days?

Additional Study *Acts 1:4; Luke 18:1; Colossians 4:2-4; Philippians 4:4-7*

Swing Thought

When your life looks and feels like the challenge of the final round of a major golf championship, face it with rejoicing, patience, and prayer. God promises that, in the end, you will be a winner.

KEY VERSE

. . . pray continually . . . (I Thessalonians 5:17)

Personal Reflection and Discussion Questions

1. Just as the area around holes 11 through 13 at the Augusta National course is called "Amen Corner" for its challenges and pitfalls, we have times like that in our lives. Do you have an "Amen Corner" in your life . . . a difficult or troublesome situation with "hazards" and a possible "bogie or worse"? Describe it.

2. How are we to pray according to I Thessalonians 3:10?

    What is lacking in your faith that you would like God to supply?

3. What does Ephesians 6:18 add to your understanding of how to pray?

4. In what ways are you challenged by these verses about prayer?

    In what ways are you frustrated?

    What can you do about these challenges and frustrations?

5. How do you hope to modify your prayer life?

Additional Study *Matthew 26:41; James 5:13-18; Mark 11:24-25; Proverbs 15:8, 29; Psalms 47:6-7; 113:1-9; I Chronicles 16:23-27; 29:13.*

Swing Thought

Pray constantly that God will be with you and direct your path as you go through the "amen corners" in the course of your life. This attitude of praise can—and will—change your life.

PART EIGHT

Dealing with the Sin
in Your Life

KEY VERSE

Nothing in all creation is hidden from God's sight. Everything is uncovered and laid bare before the eyes of him to whom we must give account. (Hebrews 4:13) (The Living Bible says: . . . nothing can be hidden from him to whom we must explain all things.)

Personal Reflection and Discussion Questions

1. How is "character laid bare" in golf?

2. In Hebrews 4:12, how is the word of God
   (a) living and active?

   (b) sharper than any two-edged sword?

   (c) piercing to the division of soul and spirit, of joints and marrow?

   (d) discerning the thoughts and intentions of the heart?

3. What does Hebrews 4:13 (Living Bible) mean when it says, "nothing can be hidden from him to whom we must explain all things"?

4. Relate Hebrews 4:12-13 to your own experience.

   (a) When has the word of God been like this to you?

   (b) How did it cut through to your innermost being and reveal something about yourself?

   (c) What passage of the Bible and/or occasion revealed this to you?

5. How can the word of God do such a thing (i.e. pierce the soul and spirit and discern the thoughts and intentions of the heart)?

Additional Study *Psalm 33:8-15; Hebrews 4:11-13; Ephesians 6:17.*

Swing Thought

When laid bare to the issue of character, where do you stand today? Are you willing to be straight with God about that, and then be honest with yourself and two or three others? Accountability to God and to those you trust is a great character booster.

KEY VERSE

I do not understand what I do. For what I want to do I do not do,
but what I hate I do. (Romans 7:15)

Personal Reflection and Discussion Questions

1. What are the "shanks" like in golf? If you have had them, describe your thoughts, feelings, and/or frustrations during that time.

2. How does that compare with the words in Romans 7:15?

   (a) Have you ever felt this way about an area of sin in your life?

   (b) Have you ever questioned yourself the way Paul did?

   (c) Will you share this experience with the study group?

3. What is the battleground that Paul is describing in Romans 7:13-25?

   (a) Who are the opponents in the battle? Between what forces is the battle being waged?

   (b) How does this description relate to your own life?

4. Romans 6:23 is a powerful summary. Meditate on it. Rephrase it in your own words.

   (a) What truth is summarized in these few words?

Additional Study *Romans 8:1-7.*

Swing Thought

Jesus wants to forgive you and give you peace this day and for eternity. Yes, you will shank the ball both on and off the course. But your Instructor is close by. Your only obligation is to pay attention to—and do—what he has to tell you.

KEY VERSE

Pride goes before destruction, a haughty spirit before a fall.
(Proverbs 16:18)

Personal Reflection and Discussion Questions

1. Have you experienced something very good in golf, followed quickly by a bad shot, hole, or holes?

   What happened? Why?

2. How does this parallel with the key verse from Proverbs?

3. What is pride, according to the Bible?

   How is it a bit different from the use of the word pride in our society?

4. Where are these three insights in our reading? What do they mean?
   (a) God hates pride and arrogance.

   (b) Pride leads to disgrace, but humility leads to wisdom.

   (c) Pride and a haughty spirit go before destruction.

5. Do you agree that "pride is the root of all sin"? Why or why not?

Additional Study *James 4:6-7; Proverbs 21:4; Mark 7:20-23*

Swing Thought

Are you relying on yourself or on God to help you in the key areas of your life? It's a question to ask yourself today—and every day.

KEY VERSE

If we confess our sins, he is faithful and just and will forgive us our sins and purify us from all unrighteousness. (I John 1:9)

Personal Reflection and Discussion Questions

1. What "move" do you make with the club (or your body) to begin the "backswing" so that you get it into the right position "at the top"?

   What "move" do you make with the club (or your body) to initiate the "downswing"?

2. What is the first move that God already made toward you to put you in a proper position with Him?

   What "move" must we make to be in a right position with God? In other words, how do we initiate the relationship he has already started?

3. What has God done that allows us to approach him to confess our sin?

4. What does the key verse say about your relationship with Jesus?

5. Why are we calling Jesus a "liar" if we say we have not sinned? (verse 10)

6. What does it mean to "walk in the light"?

Additional Study *Psalm 5:1-14; Romans 10:9-13*

Swing Thought

Confession of sin is a prayer that puts you in a right position spiritually with God. Is there something you feel you need to share with God now? He is the best listening friend you will ever have.

KEY VERSE

For the wages of sin is death, but the gift of God is eternal life in Christ Jesus our Lord. (Romans 6:23)

Personal Reflection and Discussion Questions

1. Define a "gimme." Who gives it and how? Who receives it and how? What happens if the person chooses to go ahead and putt?

2. How is that process much like the free gift Jesus offers us? What is the free gift that Jesus offers? How do we accept it? What happens if we do not accept the gift of Jesus? How is it like a "gimme" putt?

3. In the book, *What They Don't Teach You at Harvard Graduate School*, Mark McCormack (pp. 19-20) contrasts the character of people who give "gimme putts" with those who do not. Describe the character of Jesus, who gives us "life's biggest gimme." Can you find scripture that describes his character?

4. Describe exactly what Jesus gives/offers to you and others. (See Romans 5:18-21 and 3:21-26.)

   Why is it so very important that Jesus offers this gift to us?

   What price did he pay for that gift?

   What response does he hope you will give?

5. Are you prepared to describe to others the "gimme" Jesus has for them?

Additional Study You may want to review some of the other passages in Part Eight of In His Grip, "Dealing with the Sin in Your Life."

Swing Thought

God is offering you the greatest gimme of your life. Will you say "yes" to his generous offer and let him bear the burden of your sin? To say "yes" is a lot like getting a gimme from the tee box on a long par five . . . unbelievable, but true.

PART NINE

Christ is the Answer

KEY VERSE

I tell you the truth, we speak of what we know, and we testify to what we have seen, but still you people do not accept our testimony.
(John 3:11)

Personal Reflection and Discussion Questions

1. What qualities would you expect in a recruiter for God's squad?

2. How does golf provide an opportunity to share your faith in Christ?

3. How can you and others use the game of golf, and fellowship around the game of golf, as a way to share your faith in Christ?

4. What do these phrases from John 3:1-21 mean?
   (a) "no one can see the kingdom of God unless he is born again" (vs. 3)

   (b) "you must be born again" (vs. 7)

   (c) "whoever believes in him should not perish but have eternal life" (vs. 16)

   (d) "that the world might be saved through him" (vs. 17)

   (e) "this is the verdict: Light has come into the world, but men loved darkness instead of light because their deeds were evil" (vs. 19)

   (f) "what he has done has been done through God" (vs. 21)

5. How do you explain John 3:3, along with John 3:16-17, to your golfing buddy who says, "What is this stuff about being born again?"

Additional Study II Corinthians 5:16-21 (especially note verse 20); Ephesians 6:19-20; Matthew 28:16-20

Swing Thought

What is there about your life that would attract people to play with you on God's team? List two or three things you feel best describe where you are in your walk with Christ.

KEY VERSE

For the wages of sin is death, but the gift of God is eternal life in Christ Jesus our Lord. (Romans 6:23)

Personal Reflection and Discussion Questions

1. Larry Moody, chaplain to the PGA tour players, has described golf as a metaphor for life. He states that just as we are never good enough at golf to satisfy our desire for perfection, none of us are so good that we can get to heaven on our own merits. It is only in a personal relationship with Christ that we will spend eternity with our heavenly Father.

   Describe his metaphor as you would to a friend.

   How could Romans 6:23 help you explain or answer questions?

2. Carefully reflect on Romans 8:1-11 on more than one occasion during the week ahead. Even if you are familiar with this passage, jot down any new insights God seems to be pointing out to you. Share them with others and listen to the insights of other people.

3. How is the love and forgiveness of God the Father and his Son described in Romans 8:12-16?

4. What do you think and feel, knowing that God and Jesus love and forgive you in this manner?

   In what new and deeper ways do you seek to accept their love and their forgiveness within your mind and spirit?

   Ask others to pray with you about this.

Additional Study *Romans 5:18-21; Galatians 6:7-9*

Swing Thought

GOLF will either spell DISASTER or GLORY. The eternal choice is yours.

KEY VERSE

Here I am! I stand at the door and knock. If anyone hears my voice and opens the door, I will come in and eat with him, and he with me.
(Revelation 3:20)

Personal Reflection and Discussion Questions

1. Have you ever wished you had a ticket to the Masters in Augusta?

   How much would you have been willing to pay? Would you carry a sign that reads "I Need a Ticket"?

2. Why do we want to go to the Masters, or similar events like The Final Four, Super Bowl, World Series, World Cup, or the U.S. Open?

   How far do people go out of their way to attend these events?

3. What is the "ticket to heaven"? What is the cost? How do you get one?

4. Why do people not realize that they need a ticket to heaven and that it is so easy to get one?

   How can you help them to see their need and help them to "get the ticket"?

5. Do you still need your ticket to heaven? Will you accept the free ticket? From these recent readings you know you can pray to God:

   "Jesus, I believe you died on the cross as the penalty for my sins. Please come into my life now and forgive me for my sins. I ask you to take control of my life. I want you to be my Lord and Savior from this day forward."

   When you pray that prayer, you receive the ticket to heaven and you are a part of God's family. Tell a trusted friend who will understand and support you.

Additional Study *Review the passages for this study and prior studies in Part Nine: Christ is the Answer.*

Swing Thought

When you carry a sign saying, I NEED A TICKET, make sure you are asking for the ticket that will do you the most good—the only ticket, in fact, that will ultimately matter.

KEY VERSE

For whoever wants to save his life will lose it, but whoever loses his life for me will save it. (Luke 9:24)

Personal Reflection and Discussion Questions

1. Can you explain Bobby Jones' statement "To cure a slice you have to learn to aim where you don't want the ball to go"?

2. Read Luke 9:23. What does it mean for a person to

   (a) deny himself?

   (b) take up his cross daily?

   (c) follow me (Jesus)?

3. Statements of "opposites" are situations where "what actually happens in response to our actions is almost the opposite of what we expect would happen." Explain two such statements in Luke 9:24:

   (a) Whoever wants to save his life will lose it.

   (b) Whoever loses his life for me will save it.

4. What does verse 25 mean? How can a person "gain the whole world" while "losing or forfeiting himself"?

   How can you avoid this trap?

   Ask God to help you.

Additional Study *Matthew 10:34-39; 23:10-12; John 12:24-26; Mark 9:35; 10:43-45*

Swing Thought

The more we give up to God the more he gives to us. What "opposite" thinking is God asking you to consider today?

Prayer Requests & Notes

On the Green

PART TEN

God's Spirit at Work
in Us

KEY VERSE

I have labored and toiled and have often gone without sleep; I have known hunger and thirst and have often gone without food; I have been cold and naked. (II Corinthians 11:27)

Personal Reflection and Discussion Questions

Tour caddies typically perform their responsibilities with the attitude and behavior much like a "servant." They walk alongside, or just behind, the player. They stay behind to replace a divot or rake a bunker. They protect the clubs and the player from the rain with the umbrella. They wait patiently outside the clubhouse (in the rain, heat, or cold) while the players are inside eating or resting.

They lug the heavy bag around the course. They make certain it is supplied with balls, towels, extra gloves, spikes, and energy snacks. They measure distances and survey pin locations. They treat the pro with respect to his face and behind his back. They think of the player's performance as "we" and share in his success.

1. How does this compare with your relationship with Christ? What are some similarities? What are some differences?

2. How did Paul demonstrate the attitude and behavior of a servant?

3. How is it possible to be both servant and joint-heir to God's kingdom?

4. What is the most severe pain, punishment, or conditions you have encountered as a servant of Christ?

5. How does that compare to the hardships of Paul or others you have personally known?

Additional Study Romans 8:14-17; II Corinthians 6:1-10

Swing Thought

Are you a good servant of Jesus Christ? Do you find yourself willing to submit yourself to his regimen? Do you refuse to take the credit so that he can receive the glory in your life?

KEY VERSE

*But the fruit of the Spirit is love, joy, peace, patience, kindness, good-
ness, faithfulness, gentleness and self-control. Against such things
there is no law. (Galatians 5:22)*

Personal Reflection and Discussion Questions

1. The fruit of the Spirit in Galatians 5:22-23 is preceded by a contrast
    in verses 18-21. What contrasting behaviors do those verses describe?

2. Describe what these phrases from verses 16 and 18 mean: "walk by
    the Spirit" and "be led by the Spirit."

3. Describe in your own words the contrast in Galatians between "the
    works of the flesh" and "the fruit of the Spirit." Where does each of
    them come from?

    Summarize what God says about each of these two categories.

4. Which of the nine fruits of the Spirit is most evident in your life at
    this time? Which is most lacking?

5. How can we have more of the "fruit" and less of the works of the
    "flesh" in our lives?

    Pray that God will use the Holy Spirit to demonstrate more fruits of
    the Spirit in your life.

Additional Study *Ephesians 5:7-10 (could continue through verse 20);
Colossians 3:12-17; I Corinthians 13:4-7*

Swing Thought

*When we allow the Spirit of God to change us and put us to useful service,
we will begin to see the fruit of our labor.*

KEY VERSE

Finally, be strong in the Lord and in his mighty power. Put on the full armor of God so that you can take your stand against the devil's schemes. (Ephesians 6:10-11)

Personal Reflection and Discussion Questions

1. Have you ever had an experience in which someone showed you how to use your golf clubs in a totally new way?

2. Do you understand the purpose of the whole armor of God as described in verses 10 through 13 of Ephesians 6? What is the purpose?

3. What are the six parts of the armor of God and what is the unique purpose of each part?

4. Why do we need to know about and use all six pieces of armor?

5. What will happen to the believer who does not know about and use these six?

Additional Study *I Corinthians 16:13; II Corinthians 10:3-6; Romans 8:37-39*

Swing Thought

Do you know how and when to use the spiritual armor of truth, righteousness, peace, faith, salvation, and the Spirit? It's in your bag! Learn to use it when needed and appropriate.

KEY VERSE

For God did not give us a spirit of timidity, but a spirit of power, of love and of self-discipline. (II Timothy 1:7)

Personal Reflection and Discussion Questions

1. Golf requires a balance between aggressiveness and timidity.

    Are there situations where you may be too timid in your golf game?

    In what situations are you too aggressive in golf?

2. Why is it that with God's power, love, and self-discipline, we should no longer be timid in our walk through life?

3. On the other hand, in what ways can we become too aggressive in our application of God's power, love, and self-discipline?

4. Describe a situation in life where you would like to be more bold, but not overly aggressive, in serving God with his power, love, and self-discipline.

Additional Study Romans 8:12-17; John 14:25-31

Swing Thought

With God's power, love, and self-control at work in your life, you will no longer need to be timid. You can even be bold in pursuing the things that are beyond your own natural capability.

KEY VERSE

Therefore, as God's chosen people, holy and dearly loved, clothe your-selves with compassion, kindness, humility, gentleness and patience.
(Colossians 3:12)

Personal Reflection and Discussion Questions

1. By applying concepts learned earlier in this book, how do you think we learn to "clothe" ourselves with compassion, kindness, lowliness, meekness, and patience?

2. Which of the five qualities is the most difficult for you to practice?

   Describe a situation where you fell short in that area of your life.

3. Which of these five qualities do you do best in your life?

   Give an example where you did live out that quality.

4. Where would you like to better demonstrate patience? . . . in golf? . . . in life?

5. Why is patience particularly troublesome in golf? . . . in life?

Additional Study *Luke 8:15; Romans 8:24-25; 12:12; James 5:7-11*

Swing Thought

Do you need to pause for a while and do some serious reflecting today? Are you willing to slow down long enough to ask God to direct you in developing patience?

PART ELEVEN

Our Relationships

KEY VERSE

Husbands, love your wives, just as Christ loved the church and gave himself up for her. (Ephesians 5:25)
And he will go on before the Lord, in the spirit and power of Elijah, to turn the hearts of the fathers to their children . . .(Luke 1:17a)

Personal Reflection and Discussion Questions

1. Why is "Our Family Job #1"?

2. Read the sections of Ephesians 5 and 6 that apply to you in your role as a wife, husband, or child (even as a grown "child"). Seek to understand and apply it in your own life. What does it say to you?

3. Tom Lehman's occupation as a tour golf professional is demanding and could distract from his role as husband and father. How can your occupation do the same in your life?

   How do you (could you) overcome this distraction?

4. What are the excuses you tend to give for not being a better father, grandfather, husband, wife, son, or daughter? How are you going to overcome or eliminate them?

5. What else interferes with spending quality time with your family?

   How can you change that? Do not presume it cannot be changed.

Additional Study *Ephesians 5:21-6:9; Colossians 3:18-22; I Peter 3:1-7*

Swing Thought

What are your godly family responsibilities? Have you allowed fame, career, success, or time to get in the way of those responsibilities? If so, today is a good day to gain a fresh perspective on what is truly important.

KEY VERSE

And let us consider how we may spur one another on toward love and good deeds. Let us not give up meeting together, as some are in the habit of doing, but let us encourage one another . . .
(Hebrews 10:24-25)

Personal Reflection and Discussion Questions

1. Do you have someone to play golf with who encourages you? What does he/she do that is encouraging?

2. How can you encourage others on the golf course and afterwards
   (a) with positive words of encouragement?

   (b) with constructive critique?

3. Do you have someone who encourages your personal life and spiritual walk with God?

   How do you encourage and critique one another?

   How do you cultivate this relationship?

4. From Hebrews 10:23-25, what does it mean for us to
   (a) stir up one another to love and good works?

   (b) not neglect to meet with one another?

   (c) encourage one another?

5. How can you be more receptive to the encouragement you get from others at home, on the golf course and in other areas of your life?

Additional Study *Colossians 2:1-5; Ephesians 6:21-23; Philippians 2:1-11*

Swing Thought

We need to be givers and receivers of encouragement in our home, with our friends on the golf course, and with other people in our lives. With God's help, we can improve both in giving and receiving encouragement.

KEY VERSE

. . . who comforts us in all our troubles, so that we can comfort those in any trouble with the comfort we ourselves have received from God.
(II Corinthians 1:4)

Personal Reflection and Discussion Questions

1. II Corinthians 1:3-4a says that God is "the Father of compassion and God of all comfort, who comforts us in all our troubles . . ." That is very powerful, but hard to fully grasp. What does it mean to you?

2. How has God comforted you in different areas of trouble?

3. The passage goes on to say that we comfort others "with the comfort we ourselves have received from God." What does that mean?

4. Describe situations where you have been able to comfort others in an affliction which you had experienced earlier yourself.

5. How does God use people (yourself and others) to provide comfort?

Additional Study *Proverbs 17:17; II Corinthians 7:5-16; Romans 8:12-17; Colossians 1:24-29*

Swing Thought

Having "been there and done that" may be your golden opportunity to give a word of comfort to someone who is currently experiencing some "affliction" on the golf course or in the game of life.

KEY VERSE

Do not forget to entertain strangers, for by so doing some people have entertained angels without knowing it.
(Hebrews 13:2)

Personal Reflection and Discussion Questions

1. Describe some of the situations on the golf course where you can be alert to show hospitality to others . . . especially strangers.

   How would you like to show more hospitality on the golf course?

2. In what ways are we like ambassadors for Christ when we show hospitality to others?

3. How are we showing hospitality to Christ himself when we care for "the least of these"? (See Matthew 28.)

4. How might we be showing hospitality to an angel? (Hebrews 13:2)

   Do you believe you have demonstrated hospitality to someone who was an angel of the Lord?

5. Have you ever experienced the hospitality of someone who did not even know you? What was it like? Was he or she like an angel?

Additional Study Matthew 24:31-46; I Peter 1:22-25; 4:8-9; *Romans 12:9-13*

Swing Thought

Hospitality is a matter of the heart that is revealed in our actions and in our words. Hospitality to strangers is an expectation Christ has given to us.

KEY VERSE

As iron sharpens iron, so one man sharpens another.
(Proverbs 27:17)

Personal Reflection and Discussion Questions

1. What golfers help you sharpen your game? What do they do?

2. What people help you to sharpen your spiritual walk? What do they do?

3. For whom do you need to be the "iron" that helps sharpen them? How can you help sharpen them? What is the next step and when?

4. Who can be that "iron" in your life?

5. How can you allow or encourage those people to help sharpen and shape you?

Note: We each need to identify those for whom we can be "iron" and those who will be "iron" for us. The Fellowship of Christian Athletes, a local Promise Keepers group, a small group in your church, or a golf fellowship group may be a way of fulfilling this need. Max Lucado's book *On the Anvil* has helpful insights on how God wants to shape us for service in the Kingdom.

Additional Study Ephesians 5:21; 4:1-7; Galatians 5:13; Romans 15:14; I Thessalonians 5:11-15; Colossians 3:12-17

Swing Thought

We need to be "iron" to one another and allow others to be "iron" for us so we may be shaped and sharpened throughout life. Who is "iron" to you? Who is friend enough to speak the truth to you in love?

KEY VERSE

The body is a unit, though it is made up of many parts; and though all its parts are many, they form one body. So it is with Christ. For we were all baptized by one Spirit into one body—whether Jews or Greeks, slave or free—and we were all given the one Spirit to drink.
(I Corinthians 12: 12-13)

Personal Reflection and Discussion Questions

1. What is the "body of Christ" in this passage? What unites the parts?

2. How is a bag of golf clubs like the body of Christ? (See verses 15-20.)

   How does the uniqueness of each club add to the effectiveness of the entire set?

3. How is the body of Christ like these five comparisons to a bag of clubs?
   (a) As there are many unique clubs in the bag, they are still a set of golf clubs (vs. 20).

   (b) One club can't say to another, "I have no need of you" (vs. 21).

   (c) Every club must be cared for because all are needed to score well in a round of golf (vs. 25).

   (d) If one club suffers (is ineffective), all the clubs suffer (vs. 26).

   (e) If one is honored (due to very effective play in a round), then all rejoice together for they have done their job well (vs. 26).

Additional Study *Romans 12:3-8; Ephesians 4:11-13*

(Also review the study on "Balance" in Part Five.)

Swing Thought

Play a round of golf without your putter to see what it's like. It should be quite an experience. Then identify one or more people you know in the Body of Christ who are truly different from you. Can you learn to love them and respect these individuals?

PART TWELVE

Keep on Going to the Finish

KEY VERSE

I press on toward the goal to win the prize for which God has called me heavenward in Christ Jesus. (Philippians 3:14)

Personal Reflection and Discussion Questions

1. Why is perfection unattainable in golf?

2. Why is perfection unattainable in our lives and faith?
   (See Philippians 3:12.)

3. The King James Version of the Bible says Paul is pressing on toward "the mark." The Revised Standard Version calls it "the goal." What is the "mark" or "goal" that Paul is striving toward?
   (See Philippians 3:14, 8-10.)

4. What does it mean in practical everyday living for you to "press on toward the mark"? (See verse 14.)

   What is "straining forward to what lies ahead"? (See verse 13.)

5. What would it involve for you to "know him and the power of his resurrection, . . . share his sufferings, become like him in death"? What holds you back from doing that at this time?

Additional Study *I Timothy 6:11-16; II Corinthians 13:5-9; I Corinthians 3:10-23*

Swing Thought

Though perfection is unattainable, we still press on toward that mark. In your desire to be the best, never forget that you have an even higher calling—to give God your best today and always.

KEY VERSE

But seek first his kingdom and his righteousness, and all these things will be given to you as well. (Matthew 6:33)

Personal Reflection and Discussion Questions

1. After winning the 1996 U.S. Open, Steve Jones gave credit to Ben Hogan's book titled *Hogan* for encouraging him to live one step at a time. Steve's summary of the book was, "Focus in on each shot and don't worry about the outcome." Why is Steve Jones' summary such good advice?

   How can you use it in your golf game?

   How can you use that advice in your life?

2. How will God help you to live out that advice in your life?

3. How does Matthew 6:33 apply to "focusing on each shot" in your life?

4. Precisely what does Matthew 6:34 mean for your life?

5. What does Psalm 37:23-24 mean to you?

Additional Study Proverbs 6:9; 20:24; Matthew 6:25-32; Philippians 4:4-7; Psalms 18:36 and 37:23-24 (theme verses for the title In His Grip)

Swing Thought

Focus in on each shot and don't worry about the outcome. Keep your mind on one thing at a time. When you do this, the rest usually will take care of itself.

KEY VERSE

*I have fought the good fight, I have finished the race,
I have kept the faith. (II Timothy 4:7)*

Personal Reflection and Discussion Questions

1. Paul is encouraging Timothy. It is near the end of Paul's ministry, but Timothy must go on. Read II Timothy 4:1-8 as though Paul is writing to you personally. What are your thoughts and feelings?

   What do you want to do as a result of Paul's encouragement to you?

2. He says to "fulfill your ministry." What do you believe is your ministry at this time in your life?

   How can you "fulfill your ministry"?

3. How can you be sure that near the end of your life, like Paul, you will be able to say, "I have fought the good fight, . . . finished the race, . . . kept the faith"? Note: This is the theme for our book *Finishing the Course: Strategies for the Back Nine of Your Life.*

4. What does the phrase "Living In His Grip" now mean to you?

5. Which of the "Foundations for Life" seem most relevant to you as you move forward in fighting the good fight, running the race, and keeping the faith?

Additional Study *I Timothy 6:12-16; Philippians 3:12-16; 1:21-30; II Timothy 1:11-14; James 1:12*

Swing Thought

Will you stay "in his grip"? We pray you will.

Prayer Requests & Notes

APPENDIX

Starting A Golf Fellowship Group

Jim Sheard, Ph.D.

Many golf fellowship groups have formed throughout the country and on the professional golf tours. This seems to be the outgrowth of the increased popularity of golf. There is also an increased awareness among people, especially men, of the desire to fellowship and encourage one another in the faith. Golf fellowship groups are being formed among friends, in churches, groups of churches, golf ministries, sports ministries like Fellowship of Christian Athletes, and ministries devoted to men such as Christian Business Men's Club and Promise Keepers. Women's groups have also formed fellowship groups as they have seen golf as a ministry opportunity.

Many individuals have recognized the need and formed a group along with the support of their pastor or friends. The availability of *In His Grip* and our second book *Playing the Game* has been an encouragement to many individuals to get together with other golfers to fellowship and apply the Bible to life. Many of these groups and individuals have asked how to get a golf fellowship started.

We have four categories of considerations in forming a golf fellowship group: purpose, people, program (study materials), and plan (format and place). We have highlighted some of the ideas others have found helpful.

PURPOSE

First, decide what it is that you are trying to accomplish with such a group. Think about and discuss with others the reason you would like to form a golf fellowship group. The range of options may include:

1. To play golf with people who share faith in Christ.
2. To study God's word and grow in faith with others for whom golf is a common interest.
3. To reach out to others through:
    a. - playing golf together, and/or
    b. - studying God's word together in a golf-oriented environment.
The ideas that follow are primarily oriented to objective #2. These ideas will help form a nucleus from which goals #1 and #3 can also be pursued. Goal #1 is also expanded upon in our publication *Hosting a Christian Golf Event*, which is available by phone, mail, or our website.

PEOPLE

The second consideration is people—who are you going to invite to participate in your golf fellowship group (i.e. your study group)? That may be easy because there is already a natural group of people who should be invited. There may be an existing golf league in your church or perhaps there are men's or couples' groups who could be invited to an introductory meeting.

Where a group does not already exist, it may be possible to include an announcement in the church bulletin, newspaper, or Christian radio station. You may want to invite men, women, or couples from your neighborhood, several churches, or a country club. On a smaller scale, you and a few others may each have friends or acquaintances you would like to invite. That is all it would take, a handful who want to share their common bond in golf and faith.

While we may emphasize the formation of men's groups, the same comments apply as well to women and couples who share an interest in golf. Frankly, men have typically needed more encouragement in this kind of thing. Women seem to be much better at finding ways to get together to learn about the Lord and to share their ideas and feelings.

Pray about the idea, share it with others, and watch for God's leading.

PROGRAM

Another key consideration will be the material you will study together. *In His Grip* includes a total of 67 single page "devotionals." The 67 topics are grouped into twelve parts ranging in length from three to nine topics. In this handbook, the 12 themes are grouped into four sections: On the Tee, In the Fairway, Help for the Hazards, and On the Green. Each section is a bible study of 14 to 20 lessons. Most study groups find it wise to commit to doing a section over a scheduled period of several weeks. The group can then review their plans before continuing on to another section.

The benefits of using *In His Grip* and The *Player's Handbook* for a golf fellowship study are fairly obvious:
1. They are built around the common interest of golf.
2. There are questions for personal application/discussion.
3. The discussion format is easy to lead and, therefore, eases the preparation requirements for a leader/teacher.
4. The format is attractive and easy to use.
5. They highlight matters of faith important to everyone.

PLAN

Develop a plan for your fellowship group with one or two others who will help take responsibility for the planning and implementation. Questions to consider include:

1. How frequently will we meet? (Weekly, every other week, or monthly are common.)
2. Where to meet? (Coffee Shop, Clubhouse, Church, Office, Home, etc.)
3. What time of the day, day of the week, and for how long should we meet?
4. Do we include playing golf in every meeting, once a month, never, etc.?
5. How long do we intend to continue meeting? How many times do we plan to meet?
6. Will one person be the discussion leader or will we rotate that responsibility?
7. Are we open to adding new people as we continue in the study? How will we seek additional people to join us?
8. If we get too large, will we form more than one discussion group? (Usually a group of four to seven is the best for discussion.) If there is more than one discussion group meeting at the same time, you can get the entire group together before or after the small group discussions to share announcements or to wrap-up the discussion.

LEADING AN *IN HIS GRIP* GOLF FELLOWSHIP STUDY GROUP

The *Player's Handbook* helps individuals and study groups apply the foundations from *In His Grip* to their lives . . . and golf games. The individuals in an effective study group can help one another discover and apply these foundations.

The Handbook is easy for an individual or a group to follow. A group can review and discuss one of the devotional pages from *In His Grip* without a lot of preparation by the group members or discussion leader. However, the commitment and prior study of each participant will enhance the discussion.

Group discussion will also be aided by a leader who has thoughtfully prepared to lead the discussion and prayed for the group in advance. The leadership responsibilities may be assigned to one individual who is willing and capable, or it may be rotated for each lesson.

Ultimately, each member of the group shares the responsibility for the progress of the group. Therefore, it is helpful for everyone to be familiar with these "Tips."

"TIPS" FOR LEADING THE GROUP DISCUSSION

These guidelines will help the leader. It is best if all members of the group share their implementation.
1. Begin and end on time. The proposed discussion format can be easily completed in an hour. If more time is available for further discussion, socializing, or some golf activity, that can be planned and scheduled.
2. Recognize (and remind people) that this is a "discussion." The leader and participants need to recognize that it is not a lecture. Furthermore, the discussion leader is not the teacher. He/she need not, and should not, strive to impose his or her view on the group.
3. The Bible is the final reference. This is not a free forum for any teaching or ideas. The final authority is the word of God in the Bible, and we will seek to understand what it says to us about the topics under discussion. Within that framework we are all seeking to learn and to grow in our faith and understanding. We are seeking to be like Jesus and to follow His teachings for God's kingdom.
4. Read each discussion question as it is written. It is alright to clarify the question, but each question is designed to provoke thinking and discussion. Read the question and let people think and respond. Don't worry about moments of silence.
5. Don't answer your own question. Let others respond before you offer your ideas.
6. Don't feel obligated to comment on every question or topic. Avoid acting like or trying to be the final authority or have the last comment on each topic. Remember you are facilitating the discussion, not teaching the lesson.
7. Encourage more than one answer to each question. The questions are open-ended discussion questions. There is always room for more than one answer. Involve a variety of people's ideas on each question. Do not let any one person dominate the discussion or be the first to respond to every question.
8. Encourage participation from everyone. People will vary in the amount of involvement and participation they have in the discussion. But, the leader should help those who are quieter to get involved in the discussion. Watch for opportunities to ask them to add their view without putting them on the spot.
9. Keep the discussion on track. This means that you move the group through the discussion questions at an appropriate pace so that you are not bogged down on any one topic. It also means that you help the group get back to the topic and the discussion questions if the comments stray away.
10. Use follow-up questions to help enhance the discussion. Questions like these can encourage discussion:
- Can you say more about that?
- Can someone else share his or her ideas on this?
- What does our passage say about this?
- Do you have examples from your life?
- What is hardest for you in this area?
- How can you grow in this area?
- What biblical/life lessons have helped you grow in this area?

11. Do not reject anyone's answer. Do not tell anyone they are wrong or their idea has no merit. Follow-up questions can help to expand and offer alternative ideas or alternative biblical references. This can be aided with questions like: How did you come to that conclusion? What verses support your thought? Do others have thoughts on this?
12. Help if there are disagreements. Disagreements are alright, but they should not divide the group or bog down the discussion. Help people see the biblical references that will help them learn and grow. On many topics there may be differences of interpretation, but ultimately we must all seek our answers and guidance from God and His word.
13. Be a good listener. Try to be attentive to each group member. Look at each person as he/she is speaking. Try to hear what he/she is saying. Also, try to understand each person's meaning. Paraphrase or ask a follow-up question, when needed, to clarify the meaning. Show your understanding and appreciation with phrases like:
• It sounds like that has meant a lot to you.
• You would like to see this change in your life.
• That is a helpful idea for all of us.
14. Be an encourager. We are here to help each other learn and grow. We need to encourage one another to be honest, open, and searching for God's direction in our lives. At times this may include encouragement of one another during the time in between the group discussions.

SUGGESTIONS FOR... PREPARING TO PARTICIPATE IN, OR TO LEAD, THE DISCUSSION

1. Pray During the Week
  a. Pray that God will help you as a discussion leader or member.
  b. Pray for your own growth.
  c. Pray for the growth of the other members.
2. Read the Lesson
  a. Read the devotional verses (including those in the Additional Study section).
  b. Read the devotional and reflect on its meaning and application in your life.
  c. Read the Personal Reflection and Discussion questions and note your own thoughts and reactions on each question.
3. Apply the Lesson in your own life
  a. Ask God to help you grow in the application of the foundations from the Bible in your daily life.
  b. Be open to the leading of the Holy Spirit in your life as you seek to be renewed.

DISCUSSION FORMAT
IN HIS GRIP GOLF FELLOWSHIP STUDY GROUP

1. Welcome
  a. Start with a friendly atmosphere.
  b. Welcome and introduce any new people.
2. Opening prayer for guidance
3. Read the lesson (optional)
  a. Read the entire passage of scripture for the devotional.
  b. Take turns reading small portions of the lesson.
4. Discussion questions
  Discuss the four to six questions.
  a. Allocate your time so that you are typically able to do all, or most, of the discussion questions.
  b. Use follow-up questions to help encourage discussion.
  c. Use the Additional Study references to highlight or enhance the discussion of certain topics.
5. Discuss application ideas
  After completing the discussion questions, help each other identify the practical application to current life situations.
6. Pray together
  a. Share prayer requests.
  b. Share in a time of prayer.

We wish you the best in life and golf!

If you want to order resources, ask questions, offer advice, or share experiences that will help others, please feel free to write or call:

Jim Sheard, Ph.D., Co-Founder
In His Grip Resources
P. O. Box 642, Owatonna, MN 55060

1-888-899-GRIP (4747) Phone & FAX
www.in-his-grip.com

For information on instructional golf tapes, family golf schools, golf clinics and retreats, and golf training aids developed by Wally Armstrong call 1-800-YOUR MAX.

For information on speaking engagements and clinics by Wally or his golf school staff, contact Gator Golf Enterprises:

Wally Armstrong
Co-Founder In His Grip Resources and President, Gator Golf Enterprises
P.O. Box 941911
Maitland, FL 32794

PHONE 1-407-644-3398
FAX 1-407-644-9093